You Are There

Leaders

People Who Make a Difference

Reading Consultant   Linda Cornell,
Learning Resource Consultant   Indiana Department of Education

Acknowledgments:

Product Development   Gare Thompson Associates
Design   Carlos Gaudier
Production   Silver Editions
Editor/Research   Beverly Mitchell

Photo Credits:

Cover (top left, top right, bottom left, bottom right), Library of Congress; cover (center), Images © 1996 PhotoDisc, Inc.; 3 (left), John F Kennedy Library; 3 (right), Images © 1996 PhotoDisc, Inc.; 4 (top), Library of Congress; 4 (bottom left), Images © 1996 PhotoDisc, Inc.; 4 (bottom right), Library of Congress; 5 (top left), © Matthew McVay/Tony Stone Images; 5 (top right, bottom left), Images © 1996 PhotoDisc, Inc.; 5 (bottom right), Library of Congress; 6 (top left), Library of Congress; 6 (top right, bottom left), Images © 1996 PhotoDisc, Inc.; 6 (bottom right), Courtesy of the Dallas Convention & Visitors Center; 7 (all), Images © 1996 PhotoDisc, Inc.; 8 (all), Library of Congress; 9 (top left), Images © 1996 PhotoDisc, Inc.; 9 (background, top right, bottom), Library of Congress; 10 (all), Library of Congress; 11 (left), Library of Congress; 11 (center left), Corbis-Bettmann; 11 (center right, right), UPI/Corbis-Bettmann; 12 (left), UPI/Corbis-Bettmann; 12 (right), John F. Kennedy Library; 13 (left), Library of Congress; 13 (right), Images © 1996 PhotoDisc, Inc.; 14 (all), Library of Congress; 15 (left, center), Library of Congress; 15 (right), UPI/Corbis-Bettmann; 16 (left), © Robert Kusel/Tony Stone Images; 16 (right), Library of Congress; 17 (left), Library of Congress; 17 (right), Images © 1996 PhotoDisc, Inc.; 18 (left, right), Library of Congress; 18 (center), White House Historical Association; 19 (left), Library of Congress; 19 (center), Images © 1996 PhotoDisc, Inc.; 19 (right), Skrebneski/©1996 Harpo Productions, Inc.; 20 (left), Library of Congress; 20 (right), © Matthew McVay/Tony Stone Images; 21 (left), NASA; 21 (right), Images © 1996 PhotoDisc, Inc.; 22 (left), Images © 1996 PhotoDisc, Inc.; 22 (center), Underwood & Underwood/Corbis-Bettmann; 22 (right), Library of Congress; 23 (left, center), Library of Congress; 23 (top right), Images © 1996 PhotoDisc, Inc.; 23 (bottom right), NASA; 24 (left), © Ena Keo/Photographer; 24 (right), Library of Congress; 25 (left), Library of Congress; 25 (right), Images © 1996 PhotoDisc, Inc.; 26 (top center), Library of Congress; 26 (bottom center), Images © 1996 PhotoDisc, Inc.; 26 (right), © Ena Keo/Photographer; 27 (left), © Ena Keo/Photographer; 27 (center), © Terry Farmer/Tony Stone Images; 27 (right), Library of Congress; 28 (all), Library of Congress; 29 (left), Images © 1996 PhotoDisc, Inc.; 30 (center, right), Library of Congress; 31 (left), Library of Congress; 31 (center), Reuters/Corbis-Bettmann; 31 (right), Images © 1996 PhotoDisc, Inc.; 32 (top), Images © 1996 PhotoDisc, Inc.; 32 (bottom), Reuters/Corbis-Bettmann.

Library of Congress Cataloging-in-Publication Data

Thompson, Gare.
Leaders : people who make a difference / by Gare Thompson ; photographer, Martin W. Sandler.
p. cm. -- (You are there)
Summary: Provides brief information on the accomplishments of Americans who worked for social change as well as leaders in the fields of government, industry, science, art, and sports.
IBSN 0-516-20704-0 (lib. bdg.) ISBN 0-516-26056-1 (pbk.)
1. United States--Biography--Anecdotes--Juvenile literature. 2. Leadership--Anecdotes--Juvenile literature. [1. Leadership.] I. Sander, Martin W., ill. II. Title. III. Series You are there (Danbury, Conn.)
CT217.T48 1997
920.073--dc21   96-52770
                                                 CIP
                                                 AC

All Kinds of Leaders

All leaders have one thing in common. They are willing to do what they think is right. Leaders often make hard choices.

Leaders are ordinary people who do things that change people's lives. Some leaders are good at more than one thing. John F. Kennedy wrote a book and was a president.

All kinds of leaders

Lawmakers

Lawmakers are the people who make our laws. The Supreme Court makes sure the laws protect everyone. Lawmakers and the courts work together to make these decisions. They work as a team.

Change Makers

Leaders work to make changes happen. They want people to have better lives. They work to help us all feel safe and secure.

Dr. Martin Luther King Jr. led the fight for equal rights.

4

Scientists

Scientists try to improve our lives. Some scientists look for medical cures. Others search for ways to make the earth safe. Some scientists try to produce more food. Scientists work to help us lead healthier lives.

Bill Gates built a large computer software company.

Business Leaders

Business leaders run businesses that give people jobs. They think of new ways of making things. Their businesses make things we use everyday.

Dr. Jonas Salk discovered a vaccine for polio.

Sports Leaders

Sports players use their minds and bodies. They set goals and practice to reach those goals. They teach us to work together in teams or to try our best on our own.

Georgia O'Keeffe was a painter.

Artists

Artists help us see the world in new ways. They do this through painting, sculpture, acting, dance, stories, and poems. They can make us laugh or cry. They can also make us think. They help us appreciate what is around us.

The Dallas Cowboys play football.

Lawmakers
and Laws

Our country's government is based on a set of laws. Laws are made to protect us. We vote for the people who make the laws. Other people are chosen to make sure the laws are fair. Sometimes laws need to be changed to make them better.

"... all men are created equal..."
The Declaration of Independence

We the people of the United States

Signing the Declaration of Independence

The Fight for Freedom

In the 1700s, America was made up of thirteen colonies. They were ruled by the King of England. The King made the rules. But the people living in the colonies wanted to make their own rules. They decided to fight for their freedom from England.

Freedom Is Won

On July 4, 1776, the thirteen American colonies declared their freedom in a document known as the Declaration of Independence. A few years later, another document, the Constitution of the United States of America, was written to set up the new government.

Did you know?

When John Hancock signed the Declaration of Independence, he made his name very large so the King of England could see it easily.

King George III of England

The Supreme Court

Rights and Freedoms

Most of our laws are based on the Constitution. The part of the Constitution known as the Bill of Rights talks about our rights and freedoms, such as free speech. These papers were written more than two hundred years ago. They are still used today.

The Supreme Court

The three parts of our government are the Congress, the President, and the Supreme Court. Congress makes the laws. The President signs the laws. The Supreme Court decides if these laws are fair.

The Supreme Court has nine members. They are called justices. The justices are chosen by the President and approved by the Senate. The justices hear important cases. They then decide if the laws are fair.

Important Justices

Thurgood Marshall (1908-1993) was the first African-American Supreme Court justice. He served from 1967 to 1991. **Sandra Day O'Connor** (1930-   ) was the first woman on the Supreme Court. She still serves as a justice today.

Justice Sandra Day O'Connor

Campaign Poster

Time to Vote!

On the first Tuesday in November, citizens of the United States vote. All citizens over age eighteen can vote. In an election, people vote for the person they think will be the best lawmaker.

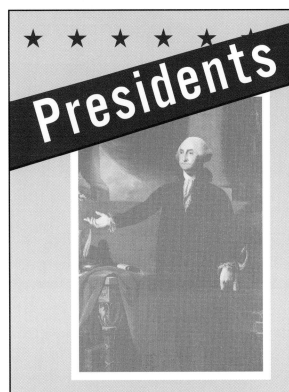

George Washington
(1732-1799)

George Washington is known as the Father of Our Country. He was a surveyor, a musician, a military leader, and our first president.

Thomas Jefferson
(1743-1826)

Thomas Jefferson wrote the Declaration of Independence and helped write the Constitution. He was an inventor, architect, and scientist. He was the first Democratic president.

Did you know?

Franklin Delano Roosevelt (1882-1945) is the only person elected president four times. After his fourth win, a law was passed to limit the presidency to two terms.

Abraham Lincoln
(1809-1865)

Soon after **Abraham Lincoln** was elected our sixteenth president, a war broke out between the North and the South over slavery. Lincoln believed that slavery was wrong. On April 15, 1865, Lincoln was shot and killed. He was the first Republican president.

A Woman for President!

Several women have run for president of the United States. The first woman to run for president was **Victoria Woodhull** in 1872. At that time, women could run for office, but they could not vote. In 1920, a law was passed allowing women to vote.

These Suffragettes want to vote!

Barbara Jordan

Barbara Jordan (1936-1996) was a lawyer who represented Texas in Congress. She worked hard to make laws that were fair to everyone. Barbara Jordan was famous for giving speeches. She had a deep and beautiful voice. She was the first African-American woman to give the main speech at a national convention.

Barbara Jordan

John F. Kennedy

(1917-1963)

Did you know?

Some elections have been very close. In 1948, a newspaper printed that Thomas Dewey was elected. But when the final votes were counted, Harry Truman was the president!

Learn More About:

Lawmakers

Books

1. Brenner, M. **Abe Lincoln's Hat.** 1994. Random House.

2. Sullivan, G. **Facts and Fun About the Presidents.** 1986. Scholastic.

Online Site

U.S. Congress
http://policy.net
Learn about the U. S. Congress and how it works.

John Fitzgerald Kennedy was born on May 29, 1917, in Brookline, Massachusetts. He believed that you must be fair to all people.

At 43, Kennedy was the youngest man elected president. On the day he became president, he said, "...ask not what your country can do for you--ask what you can do for your country." He worked hard for freedom, liberty, and peace in the world. His presidency was cut short when he was shot. He died on November 22, 1963.

Change Makers

"I have a dream that one day this nation will rise up and live out the true meaning of its creed: We hold these truths to be self–evident, that all men are created equal."

Dr. Martin Luther King Jr.

The United States of America was founded by people who wanted everyone to be treated fairly. Over the years, many people have worked hard to keep us free. These leaders make changes happen. They change how people think about each other. They work alone and with others to make life fair for all.

Time to make some changes

Working for Freedom

Frederick Douglass (1817-1895) was born a slave in Maryland. He wanted to be free. In 1838, he escaped to New York. He changed his name so his owner would not be able to find him. He started speaking and writing against slavery. He was afraid of being found so he went to England. There he saved enough money to buy his freedom. He returned to the United States as a free man. He continued to speak against slavery until he died.

Frederick Douglass

Women and the Vote

Susan B. Anthony (1820-1906) was a leader in the fight for women to vote. She published a magazine about rights for women. In 1920, the Nineteenth Amendment to the Constitution was passed. It allowed women to vote.

Susan B. Anthony

Did you know?

A one-dollar United States coin honors Susan B. Anthony. People collect these special coins.

Helen Keller

Helping Others

Helen Keller (1880-1968) became blind and deaf after a childhood illness. Annie Sullivan, her teacher, helped Helen learn the meaning of words. She learned to read, write, and speak. With the help of her teacher, Helen Keller went to college. Later, Helen and Annie gave many speeches and wrote books together. Helen Keller proved that all people could succeed.

Rosa Parks going to jail

César Chávez

Did you know?

Wilma Mankiller (1945-   ) was the first woman to become chief of the Cherokee Nation, a large Native American tribe.

Wilma Mankiller with President Reagan

Civil Rights

Rosa Parks (1913-   ) lived in Montgomery, Alabama. In 1955, African-Americans had to move to the back of city buses if white people got on. On December 1, 1955, Rosa Parks decided that she would not give up her seat for a white person. She was arrested! Her action started the fight for equal treatment for all people, called the civil rights movement.

Fair Pay for Workers

César Chávez (1927-1993) was a farm worker and labor union leader. He led farm workers in their fight to win voting rights, clean housing, toilets, and safe drinking water from farm owners. César Chávez helped farm workers get respect and fair pay for their hard work.

Carol Moseley-Braun

Did you know?

Carol Moseley-Braun (1947-) became the first African-American woman elected to the Senate when she won the 1993 election in Illinois.

Learn More About:

Change Makers

Books

1. Bradby, Marie. **More Than Anything Else**. Ill. C. K. Soentpiet. 1995. Orchard Books.

2. Celsi, T. **Rosa Parks and the Montgomery Bus Boycott**. 1991. Milbrook.

Online Site

Smithsonian Institution
http://www.si.edu
Investigate many leaders in the libraries, museums, and galleries of the Smithsonian.

MEET:

Martin Luther King Jr.

(1929-1968)

"I have a dream . . . ." Many of us recognize this famous quote by Dr. Martin Luther King Jr. Dr. King was a minister. He believed that it was not fair to have different rules for different people. He thought unfair laws had to be changed. He organized meetings and marches. Thousands of people came to help change the laws.

Dr. King believed so strongly in civil rights that he sacrificed his life. He was shot and killed on April 4, 1968. Today, because of the leadership shown by Dr. King, we all live by the same rules.

Business Leaders

"Growing up, books were my friends . . .
I want to get the whole country reading."

Oprah Winfrey, 1996

The Boston Public Library

Leaders in business affect our daily lives in many ways. Their businesses make the goods and provide the services that we use every day. They create jobs. They work to develop new products to make our lives better.

Many leaders, many products

Making a Book

This book was written by a person using a computer. It was designed by a person using another computer. The photos were taken using modern cameras. The book was printed using automatic printing methods. The book was shipped from a new automated warehouse. This is how leaders in business and industry work together to make a product.

This is an early printing press.

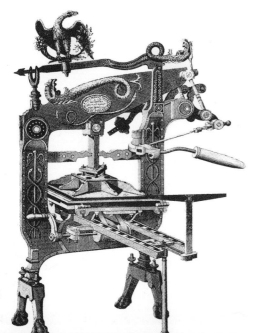

Early Printer and Inventor

Benjamin Franklin (1706-1790) learned to be a printer while working with his brother. He wrote and printed *Poor Richard's Almanac* by hand. He also became a scientist and an inventor. He invented the lightning rod, a stove, and eyeglasses. Later in his life, he became an important statesman.

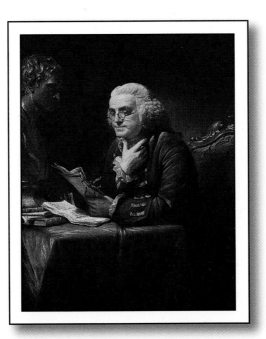

Benjamin Franklin

From Steel Mills to Libraries

Andrew Carnegie (1835-1919) built a steel empire. He worked in a factory instead of going to school. He worked hard and became vice president of a company. Carnegie saved his money and formed a new steel company. Andrew Carnegie was a leader in the steel industry. He used his money to do good things for people.

Andrew Carnegie

Did you know?

Andrew Carnegie donated money to build 2,800 public libraries. He declared, "to die wealthy would be a crime."

From a Mouse to a Park

Walt Disney (1901-1966) was an artist who combined cartooning with animation. He made movies using animals, such as Oswald the Rabbit, Mickey Mouse, and Donald Duck. In later movies, he combined live actors with animated characters. In the 1950s, he opened an amusement park called Disneyland. Today the Disney company runs several amusement parks, owns a television network, and still makes movies.

Good fast food

Billions of Burgers

Ray Kroc (1902-1984) had a job selling milkshake machines. Two of his customers, Mac and Dick McDonald, owned a restaurant that sold tasty and cheap meals in minutes. Kroc made a deal with them to open more restaurants using their name and their assembly-line system. The McDonalds restaurant chain has been growing ever since 1955.

Television Host and Businesswoman

Oprah Winfrey (1954-   ) had a difficult childhood, but she always believed in herself. At twenty-two, she became the host of a local television news program. Soon she had her own program. Today she is the host of an international television show. She and her guests discuss important issues. Many authors go on her show to talk about their new books. Oprah Winfrey is a successful businesswoman.

Walt Disney

Oprah Winfrey

19

Henry Ford (1863-1947) built a factory to make cars. He thought the cars should all be one color, black!

Henry Ford

GENTLEMEM OUR COUNTRY

Learn More About:

Business Leaders

Books

1. Kalman, Bobbie. **How a Book Is Published**. 1995. Crabtree.

2. Saltzberg, Barney. **This Is a Great Place for a Hot Dog Stand**. 1995. Hyperion.

Online Site

Ultraseek http://guide.infoseek.com. Access all kinds of facts using this search tool.

MEET:

Bill Gates
(1955-)

Bill Gates was born in Seattle, Washington. In school, he learned to use computers. Soon he spent all his time in the computer center. When he was fourteen, he started a company using computers to monitor traffic.

In 1973, Gates went to Boston to attend Harvard University and study law. But his friend told him about an idea that changed their lives. A new small computer had been built, but it needed software to make it run. So Bill Gates and his friend formed a company called Microsoft to produce software. Today Microsoft is the largest software company in the world.

Science Leaders

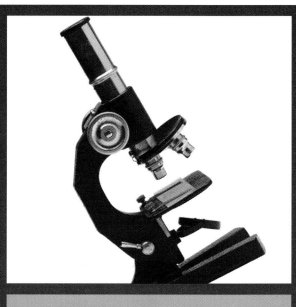

"That's one small step for a man, one giant leap for mankind."

Neil Armstrong,
first person to stand on the moon, 1969

Leaders in science work hard to make our lives safer, healthier, and easier. They work hard to make the Earth safe. They find ways to keep the environment clean. They discover cures for diseases. They invent machines to help us work, live, and play.

Protecting our environment and our lives

Fighting a Terrible Disease

Not so long ago, a disease called polio left many children paralyzed for life. Lakes and swimming pools were closed because the polio virus spread so easily. In 1954, **Dr. Jonas Salk** (1914-1995), a medical research doctor, discovered a vaccine to prevent polio. Another researcher, **Dr. Albert Sabin** (1906-1993), found a similar vaccine for polio. Today there are very few new cases of polio when the vaccines are used.

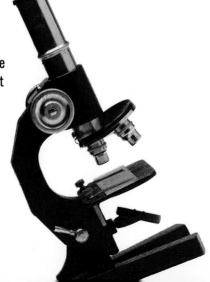

The microscope is an important research tool.

Keeping the Air Clean

Rachel Carson (1907-1964) was a scientist and a writer. She wrote a book, *The Silent Spring*, which told of the dangers of using chemicals like DDT to get rid of pests. DDT also killed birds and small animals. Carson thought it could make people sick, too. Rachel Carson warned everyone about these dangers. The use of DDT and other harmful chemicals was stopped.

Rachel Carson

Alexander Graham Bell

A Hearing Aid

Words and sounds were very important to **Alexander Graham Bell** (1847-1922) as he was growing up. As a young man, he taught deaf people to speak. He searched for a way to help deaf people by making a hearing aid. His experiments led to the invention of the telephone.

Lighting Our World

Imagine what your life would be like without electric light. **Thomas Alva Edison** (1847-1931) was a leader in the invention and use of electric lights. Modern electric lightbulbs use a wire, or filament, for the light source. Earlier lamps burned oil or gas to make light.

Thomas Alva Edison

New Crops for Farmers

George Washington Carver (1864-1941) was a scientist who tried to find better ways to grow crops. He wanted to help cotton farmers improve their soil. He found hundreds of new uses for the peanut and the sweet potato. Planting these crops helped make soil richer.

George Washington Carver

Shannon Lucid with fellow astronauts

Living in Space

Shannon Lucid (1943-) was always interested in science. In college she took flying lessons. She wanted to be a pilot. There were few jobs for women pilots, so she got a job as a chemist. In 1978, she entered the astronaut training program. In 1985, she spent a week on a space shuttle. In 1996, she spent 188 days on a Russian space station.

Did you know?

Garrett Morgan (1877-1963) liked fixing machines and experimenting with chemicals. He invented a hood to protect firemen. He also invented the gas mask and traffic signal.

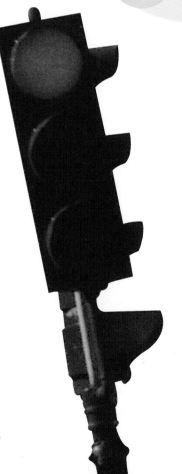

Learn More About:

Science Leaders

Books

1. Horenstein, Henry. **My Mom's a Vet**. 1994. Candlewick Press.

2. Kramer, S. **Apollo 13: Life in Space**. 1995. G. P. Putnam's Sons.

CD-ROM

The InventorLabs. 1996. Houghton Mifflin Interactive. Enter the worlds of Edison, Bell, and Watt.

Dr. Jonas Salk

(1914-1995)

As a college student, Jonas Salk worked in a research laboratory. He liked the work and decided to go to medical school. He became a medical researcher and developed a vaccine for polio that was given to two million young school children. This first test was a success, and Salk became a hero. The vaccine was made available to everyone.

Art and Artists

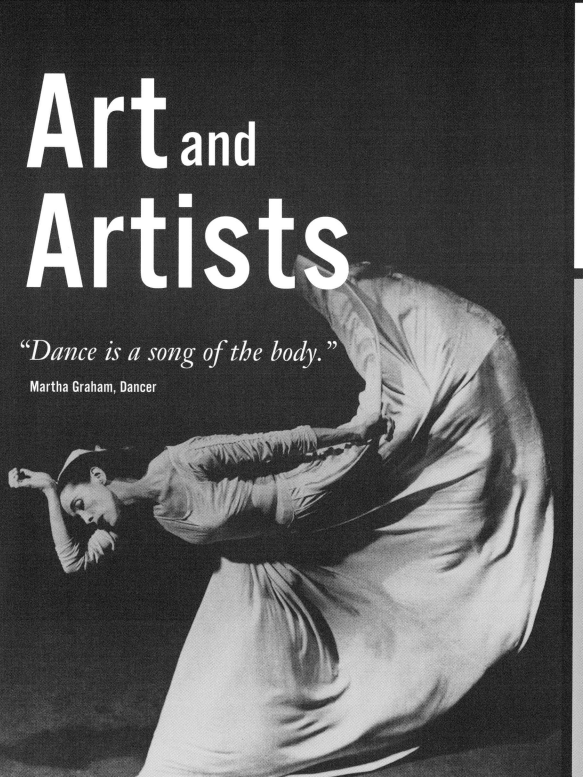

"Dance is a song of the body."
Martha Graham, Dancer

We do not spend all of our time at work or at school. We play with friends, we color and draw, we read books, we go to museums, we see movies, and we watch television.

Leaders in the arts make our world beautiful. They create paintings, music, dance, and books. Artists make us think about our world.

Georgia O'Keeffe

John Hancock Tower in Boston

Making Movie Magic

Actors and writers are important to movies. But sometimes special effects are what make a movie exciting. **Steven Spielberg** and **George Lucas** are two directors who are well known for movies that use special effects. They use computers to create the special effects.

Coloring Our World

Georgia O'Keeffe (1887-1986) is best known for her wonderful paintings of flowers. She painted huge flowers on large canvases. She was a leader in the way she used strong, clear colors.

Buildings and More Buildings

I. M. Pei (1917-   ), the architect, is a leader in the field of building design. He showed the way for today's architects by using interesting new building shapes. He designed a glass building in Boston. People thought it would not last, but it has. He has created many buildings for museums, libraries, offices, and hotels. Now others copy his style.

Got to Move!

Alvin Ailey (1931-1989) wrote poetry and took dance lessons. He studied to be a teacher, but he continued to dance. Ailey became a dance teacher and choreographer. He used dance styles and dancers from many cultures.

Alexander Calder's *Flamingo*

Reading an interesting book

A Good Book

Everyone has a favorite book. It is fun to curl up with a book and read it. Or share it with a friend.

Maurice Sendak (1928-) is a famous children's author and illustrator. Children love his book *Where the Wild Things Are* because it tells about a little boy and his adventures. Thanks to him we now have many stories about children and their everyday fears and dreams.

Shapes in Our Lives

Alexander Calder (1898-1976) was a sculptor who made exciting and amusing shapes out of metal. Calder said, "I paint with shapes." Today many of his sculptures can be found in buildings, gardens, and museums.

Did you know?

Gloria Estéfan (1957-) came to this country from Cuba. She is a singer and songwriter who has won many music awards. She also works hard to help needy people.

Alvin Ailey with members of his company

27

Did you know?

John Williams (1932-)
is a music composer and
conductor. He composes
music for television and
movies, including most
Steven Spielberg movies.

Learn More About:

Artists

Books

1. DePaola, T. **Art Lesson**. 1994. G. P.
Putnam's Sons.

2. Johnson, Angela. **Shoes Like Miss
Alice's**. Ill. K. Page. 1995. Orchard Books.

Video

Bach's Fight for Freedom. 1995.
Sony Classical.
An independent young boy reluctantly
becomes assistant to frustrated young
composer Johann Sebastion Bach.

28

MEET:

Steven Spielberg

(1947-)

Steven Spielberg was born on December 18, 1947. When he was five years old, he saw a movie, *The Greatest Show on Earth*, which led him to making movies. He started making movies of his family and his neighbors. Soon, he made all kinds of movies and entered film-making contests.

Steven Spielberg studied hard to learn his trade. He directed shows for television. Next, he made a movie, *The Sugarland Express*. Later, he made *Jaws*, *Raiders of the Lost Ark*, *The Color Purple*, and *Jurassic Park*. In 1993, he won an Academy Award for directing *Schindler's List*. He once said, "I dream for a living."

Sports Leaders

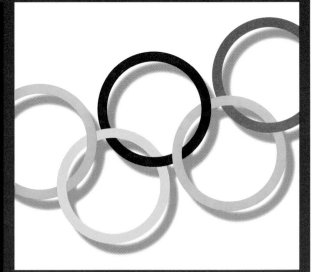

"Take me out to the ball game,
Take me out with the crowd.
Buy me some peanuts and Cracker Jack,
I don't care if I never get back."

Song by Albert Von Tilzer and Jack Norworth, 1908

The Olympic Games always begin with the lighting of the Olympic flame, in honor of the Olympics held in ancient Greece. The parade of athletes into the Olympic stadium is very exciting.

Most of us enjoy sports. We play soccer, baseball, tennis, and volleyball. We ice skate and do gymnastics. It takes practice to be a great athlete.

Gold medals and professional sports

The Olympic Games

The first Olympic Games were held more than 2,000 years ago in Greece. Those original games are still remembered by the lighting of the Olympic torch at the beginning of each Olympiad. The Olympic Games have been held every four years since 1896.

Did you know?

Since 1896, the Olympic Games have only been canceled twice, during World War I and World War II.

Gold Medal Winners

Bonnie Blair, a speed skater, competed in 1988, 1992, and 1994 and won five gold medals. Another speed skater, **Dan Jansen**, won a gold medal in 1994. It was his third try for Olympic gold.

Carl Lewis won the long jump in 1996 at age 35. He has competed in four Olympic Games since 1980. He has won a total of nine gold medals.

Carl Lewis

Gymnast **Kerri Strug** helped her team win a gold medal in 1996 even though she sprained her ankle landing her first vault. In pain, she continued, and her team won the competition.

In 1972, a swimmer, **Mark Spitz**, won seven gold medals, the most medals won by one person in the same Olympic Games. He also won two gold medals in 1968.

Amy Van Dyken became the first woman to win four gold medals for swimming, at the 1996 Olympic Games.

Mark Spitz

Professional Sports Stars

Jackie Robinson (1919-1972) was the first African-American to play baseball for a major league team. In 1947, he started playing with the Brooklyn Dodgers. He broke the "color barrier" that had existed until then in professional baseball. Today, the game of baseball is open to any skilled player. Jackie Robinson led the way for others to follow.

Jackie
Robinson

Kristi Yamaguchi won a gold medal in figure skating at the 1992 Olympic Games. Today she is a professional ice skater. She is known for her precision and grace.

Kristi Yamaguchi

Eldrick "Tiger" Woods is the youngest golfer and only African-American to win the U.S. Amateur title — three times! Woods' father began teaching him to play golf when he was only ten months old. Tiger carried a cut-off golf club with him everywhere. Experts say he is "the most important player to enter the game in fifty years."

Did you know?

Swimmer Amanda Beard was only fourteen when she won silver and gold medals for swimming. She took her teddy bear to the pool with her for good luck.

Everyone Wants to Play Soccer

Soccer is one of the fastest-growing sports in the United States. In 1996, Major League Soccer kicked off its first season. The ten teams in the league each play 32 games. Soccer is played by 120 million people in 150 countries. In the United States, 13 million kids play soccer.

Jackie Joyner-Kersee

(1962-)

Jackie Joyner was born on March 3, 1962, in East St. Louis, Missouri. Growing up, Jackie danced, ran track, played baseball and volleyball, and won high grades in school. In college, her coach was Bob Kersee. He helped her to compete in the heptathlon, which includes seven track and field events.

Jackie Joyner-Kersee won Olympic medals in 1984, 1988, 1992, and 1996. She works hard to be a good athlete. She also works hard for children at the Jackie Joyner-Kersee Community Foundation in East St. Louis.

Did you know?

Duke Kohanamoku (1890-1968), a swimmer from Hawaii, competed in four Olympic Games. He won medals each time. Duke Kohanamoku was also the first surfboarder to use the long board of his Royal Hawaiian ancestors.

Learn More About:

Sports Leaders

Books

1. Christopher, Matt. **Fighting Tackle**. 1995. Little, Brown.

2. Gutelle, Andrew. **Baseball's Best: Five True Stories**. 1990. Random House.

Video

The Big Green. 1995. Disney. An English exchange teacher tries to teach the game of soccer to a group of Texas grade-schoolers.

32